Ed Franklin

Wood Pellet Smoker and Grill

Cookbook

The Ultimate Guide to Master Your Wood Pellet Grill

Table of Contents

Core Elements of Smoking

There are six essential elements of smoking.

1- Preferred Wood Pellet chips: Chip of Preferred Wood Pellets are used as a fuel either alone or in combination with charcoals. In addition, these chips add fantastic flavor to the meat. Therefore, chips of Preferred Wood Pellet should only be used which suits best to the meat.

2- Smoker: There are basically four choices from which a smoker should be the pick. The choices are an electric smoker, charcoal smoker, gas smoker and pellet smoker. Each has its own advantages and downsides.

3- Smoking time: Smoking time is essential for perfect of meat cuts. It is the time when the internal Smoke Temperature reaches its desired values. It may take 2 hours up to more than two weeks.

4- Meat: The star of the show is meat that needs to be more tender, juicy, and flavorful after smoking. Make sure, the meat you sure have fat trimmed from it. In addition, it should complement the Preferred Wood Pellet of chips.

5- Rub: Rubs, mixture or salt and spices, add sweetness and heat to the meat. They should be prepared in such a way that all types of flavor should be balanced in the meat.

6- Mops: Mops or liquid is often used during smoking meat. It adds a little bit flavor to the meat and maintains tenderness and moisture throughout the smoking process.

Pork

1 Stuffed Pork Crown Roast

Preparation Time: 10 hours and 15 minutes

Cooking Time: 3 hours 30 minutes

Servings: 1

Smoke Temperature: 225°F, 375°F

Preferred Wood Pellet: Hickory or Apple

Ingredients:

12-14 ribs or 1 Snake River Pork Crown Roast

Apple cider vinegar - 2 tbsp

Apple juice - 1 cup

Dijon mustard - 2 tbsp

Salt - 1 tsp

Brown sugar - 1 tbsp

Freshly chopped thyme or rosemary - 2 tbsp

Cloves of minced garlic - 2

Olive oil - ½ cup

Coarsely ground pepper - 1 tsp

Your favorite stuffing - 8 cups

Directions:

Set the pork properly in a shallow roasting pan on a flat rack. Cover both ends of the bone with a piece of foil.

To make the marinade, boil the apple cider or apple juice on high heat until it reduces to about half its quantity. Remove the content from Preferred Wood Pellet and whisk in the mustard, vinegar, thyme, garlic, brown sugar, pepper, and salt. Once all that is properly blended, whisk in the oil slowly.

Use a pastry brush to apply the marinade to the roast. Ensure that you coat all the surfaces evenly. Cover it on all sides using plastic wrap. Allow it to sit for about 60 minutes, until the meat has reached room Smoke Temperature.

Currently, feel free to brush the marinade on the roast again. Cover it and return it to the refrigerator until it is time to cook it. When you are ready to cook it, allow the meat to reach room Smoke Temperature, and then put in on the pellet grill. Ensure that the grill is preheated for about 15 minutes before you do.

Roast the meat for 30 minutes, and then reduce the Smoke Temperature of the grill. Fill the crown loosely with the stuffing and mound it at the top. Cover the stuffing adequately with foil. You can also bake the stuffing separately alongside the roast in a pan.

Roast the pork thoroughly for 90 more minutes. Get rid of the foil and continue to roast the stuffing for 30-90 minutes until the pork reaches an internal Smoke Temperature of 150 degrees Fahrenheit. Ensure that you do not touch the bone of the meat with the Smoke Temperature probe or you will get a false reading.

Remove the roast from the grill. Allow it to rest for around 15 minutes so that the meat soaks in all the juices. Remove the foil covering the bones. Leave the butcher's string on until you are ready to carve it. Now, transfer it to a warm platter, carve between the bones, and enjoy!

2 BBQ Baby Back Ribs

Preparation Time: 30 minutes

Cooking Time: 6 hours 15 minutes

Servings: 1

Smoke Temperature: 225°F, 375°F

Preferred Wood Pellet: Hickory or Apple

Ingredients:

Baby back pork ribs - 2 racks

Divided apple juice - ½ cup

Yellow mustard - ⅓ cup

BBQ sauce - 1 cup

Worcestershire sauce - 1 tbsp

Warmed honey - ⅓ cup

Dark brown sugar - ½ cup

Pork and poultry rub

Directions:

Remove the silver skin membrane from the ribs from the bone side if your butcher has not done so already. You can do that by using the tip of a screwdriver or a butter knife over a middle bone underneath the membrane. To ensure a firm grip, use paper towels, and then simply tear off the membrane.

In a small bowl, combine ¼ cup of apple juice, the mustard, and the Worcestershire sauce. Reserve the rest of the juice. Thinly spread the mixture on both sides of the pork ribs and season them with the pork and poultry rub.

Once you are ready to cook them, preheat the pellet grill by setting it to a Smoke Temperature of 180 degrees Fahrenheit for about 15 minutes with the lid closed.

Smoke the ribs for about 3 hours, meat-side up. Place the ribs on a rimmed baking sheet. Increase the Smoke Temperature of the grill to 225 degrees Fahrenheit.

Tear off 4 sheets of long, heavy-duty aluminum foil. Top them with one of the racks of ribs and then pull all the sides up to ensure that the liquid stays enclosed.

Smoke half of the brown sugar that is on the rack and top it with the remaining apple juice and half of the honey. If you want even more tender ribs, you can be liberal with the apple juice.

Place another piece of foil on the top and then crimp the edges tightly so that there is no leakage. Repeat the same process with the remaining ribs.

Return all the foiled ribs back to the grill. Cook them for another 2 hours.

Remove the foil from the ribs and brush both sides with the BBQ sauce. Discard the foil and arrange the ribs directly on the grill grate.

Continue grilling them for anywhere between 30-60 minutes until the sauce solidifies.

Allow the ribs to rest for a few minutes before enjoying them!

3   Pork Tenderloin

Preparation Time: 7 Minutes

Cooking Time: 90 Minutes

Servings: 5

Smoke Temperature: 225°F, 375°F

Preferred Wood Pellet: Hickory or Apple

Ingredients:

1 Pork tenderloin GMG Pork Rub

1 Cup of Teriyaki Sauce

Directions:

You can use 1 to two pork tenderloins. Generously rub the pork tenderloins with the Green Mountain Pork Rub and let it stand aside for about 4 to 24 hours.

Set your Smoker grill at 320°F (160°C) and when the grill reaches the Smoke Temperature you are looking for, place in the tenderloin and baste both the sides with a sweet marinade like the Teriyaki sauce

Cook for about 1 and ¼ hours while turning frequently or just until the internal Smoke Temperature displays at least 165° F.

Be careful not to overcook the tenderloin because it may lead to obtaining a dry meat.

Serve and enjoy your dish!

4 Apple Orange Pork Loin Roast

Preparation Time: 5 minutes

Cooking Time: about 42 minutes

Servings: 6

Smoke Temperature: 225°F, 375°F

Preferred Wood Pellet: Hickory or Apple

Ingredients:

Peppercorns—6

Pork loin—1 5lb.

roast Orange juice—½ cup

Lemon—1, halved

Kosher salt—½ cup

Ice water—1 cup

Fennel seeds—½ tsp.

Brown sugar—¼ cup

Olive oil—2 tbsps.

Pepper flakes—½ tsp.

Garlic—3 cloves

Pepper and salt—as required

Apple juice—½ cup

Bay leaves 2

For the sauce:

Cognac—1 cup

Butter—2 tbsps.

Pepper flakes—½ tsp.

Sugar—1 cup

Minced garlic—½ tsp.

Apple juice—½ cup

Lemon—1, halved

Shallot—1, sliced thinly

Orange juice—½ cup

Fennel seeds—½ tsp.

Fresh figs—1 pint, quartered

Ice water—1 cup

Directions:

In a large enough pot, prepare a mixture of brown sugar, salt, bay leaves, garlic, lemon, peppercorns, pepper flakes, fennel seeds, orange juice, and apple. Heat and simmer to dissolve sugar and salt.

Transfer the mixture to a container with ice water and refrigerate.

In the cooled brine, add pork roast and submerge. Refrigerate for 8–12 hours.

Take out the roast, rinse it, and use paper towels to pat dry.

Use olive oil to coat the roast and season with pepper and salt.

Prepare your Smoker-Grill by preheating it to a high Smoke Temperature as per factory method Close the top lid and leave for 12–18 minutes.

Roast the meat on the grilling grate for about 23–26 minutes until the internal Smoke Temperature reaches 140°F.

Remove and allow the meat to cool before slicing.

Combine all ingredients for the sauce and heat in butter in a large enough pan. Simmer for about 20–30 minutes to reach desired thickness. Pour the sauce over the sliced pork roast. Your dish is ready to be served.

5 Pork Bone-In Chops with Rosemary and Thyme

Preparation Time: 8 minutes

Cooking Time: about 52 minutes

Servings: 6

Smoke Temperature: 225°F, 375°F

Preferred Wood Pellet: Hickory or Apple

Ingredients:

Butter—2 tbsps.

Pork—4 chops, bone-in

Rosemary—1 sprig

Thyme—2 sprigs

Pork rubs—according to taste

Directions:

Prepare your Smoker-Grill by preheating it to a Smoke Temperature of about 180°F. Close the top lid and leave for 12–18 minutes.

Use pork rub to coat the chops properly.

Transfer to the grilling grate and let the chops smoke for about 35–40 minutes. This should bring the internal Smoke Temperature to 130°F.

Remove and set aside the chops so they can cool down.

Increase the Smoke Temperature of the smoker-grill to high and let the grilling grate preheat.

In a cast iron pan, combine the herbs, butter, and pork chops.

Sear the chops, 3–5 minutes on each side.

Remove and let the chops cool for about 8–10 minutes.

Your dish is ready to be served.

6 Pork Ribs Smoked with Pomegranate Sauce

Preparation Time: 48 minutes

Cooking Time: about 4 hours

Servings: 6

Smoke Temperature: 225°F, 375°F

Preferred Wood Pellet: Hickory or Apple

Ingredients:

Bay leaves 2

Pork ribs—2 racks of baby back

Cinnamon sticks 2

Allspice berries—2 tbsps.

Onion—1

Salt—½ cup

Whole peppercorns—2 tbsps.

Garlic—1 head, halved

For the sauce:

Apple cider—1 cup

Pomegranate molasses 1/3 cup

Garlic powder—1 tsp.

Allspice—1 tsp., freshly ground

Small onion 1

Salt—½ tsp.

Cinnamon—½ tsp.

Pomegranate juice—½ cup

Black pepper—¼ tsp., ground freshly

Onion powder—1 tsp.

Brown sugar—1 cup

Cilantro—fresh

Directions:

Prepare the brine by combining water with bay leaves, garlic, allspice berries, onion, cinnamon sticks, peppercorn, and salt. Boil and then let the mixture cool.

Submerge the pork rib racks in the brine mixture. Cover and leave for 12–24 hours.

Combine all the ingredients for the sauce and simmer everything for about 30–32 minutes in a large enough saucepan. Set aside to let it cool. Then, transfer the mixture to your blender or a food processor to achieve the desired consistency.

Remove the ribs and use paper towels to pat dry.

Prepare your Smoker grill by preheating it to a Smoke Temperature of about 180°F. Close the top lid and leave for 12–18 minutes.

Put the bone section of the rib on the grilling grate. Smoke for about 2–3 hours.

Increase the Smoke Temperature to 375°F and cook the ribs for 60 minutes, coating regularly with the pomegranate sauce.

Remove and garnish with cilantro when serving.

7 Hot and Tender Pork Sausage Balls

Preparation Time: 55 minutes

Cooking Time: about 1 hour

Servings: 8

Smoke Temperature: 225°F, 375°F

Preferred Wood Pellet: Hickory or Apple

Ingredients:

For the meatballs:

Whole milk—½ cup

Pork sausage—½ lb., mild, ground

Ground beef—2 ¼ lbs.

Egg—1

Chili powder—2 tsps.

Breadcrumbs—1 cup

Hot sauce—1 tsp.

For the sauce:

Kosher salt

Olive oil—1 tbsp.

Water—1 cup

Ancho chili—1 tsp., powdered

Yellow onion 1/2, diced

Ketchup—2 cups

Brown sugar—1 ½ cups

Garlic—1 clove, minced

Apple cider—3 tbsps.

Directions:

In a large enough mixing bowl, mix the ground sausage, beef, and breadcrumbs.

In a different bowl, prepare a mixture of milk, hot sauce, and egg. Combine with the sausage mixture and add pepper, salt, and chili powder.

Prepare meatballs and place them on aluminum foil.

Prepare the Smoker grill by preheating it to a Smoke Temperature of about 180°F. Close the top lid and leave for 12–15 minutes.

Put the meatballs in a cast iron pan and transfer to the grilling grate meatballs to smoke for about 48–60 minutes.

Heat oil in a large enough saucepan and cook onion along with the available garlic. Add salt and cook while stirring for about 7–8 minutes. Mix chili powder and keep cooking for another minute or so. Mix brown sugar and simmer slowly to dissolve it completely.

Combine apple cider and ketchup. Simmer this sauce for about 16-20 minutes to achieve the desired consistency.

Remove the pan of smoked meatballs and pour the prepared sauce over them.

Increase the Smoke Temperature of the smoker-grill to about 300°F.

Cook the meatballs for about 35–45 minutes. Remove and serve with more sauce.

8 Pepper Jelly Pork Ribs

Preparation Time: 22 minutes

Cooking Time: about 4 hours

Servings: 6

Smoke Temperature: 225°F, 375°F

Preferred Wood Pellet: Hickory or Apple

Ingredients:

Sake—½ cup

Pork ribs—2 racks of baby back, remove the membrane

Garlic—4 cloves, crushed

Orange juice—½ cup

BBQ rub—4 tbsps.

Fresh ginger—1 thumb, sliced

Brown sugar—½ cup

Hoisin sauce—1 cup

Scallions—6, sliced

Cayenne pepper—½ tsp.

Soy sauce—½ cup

For the glaze:

Apple cider—½ cup

Pepper jelly—1 can of 10 oz.

Sesame seeds—toasted

Directions:

Prepare the Smoker grill by preheating it to a Smoke Temperature of about 180°F for smoking.

Use the BBQ rub to coat the pork ribs and smoke on a pan on the grilling grate for about 60 minutes.

Remove and put the ribs on high-quality aluminum foil.

Increase the Smoke Temperature of the smoker-grill to about 300°F.

Prepare a mixture of soy sauce, hoisin sauce, orange juice, sake, cayenne, and brown sugar. Dissolve the sugar and add ginger and garlic.

Pour the prepared mixture over the pork ribs. Cover and seal the pan with aluminum foil.

Cook for around 3–4 hours. Remove and let the ribs rest.

Use the cooking juices collected in the pan in the preparation of the sauce. Transfer the cooking juices to a skillet and add apple cider and pepper jelly. Boil and then simmer to achieve the desired thickness.

Use a large sharp knife to cut slices of meat from the pork ribs.

Transfer the slices to the grilling grate and glaze with the thick sauce that was prepared earlier.

Cook for about 6–12 minutes.

Your dish is ready to be served.

9 Pork Neck and Northwest Bean Soup

Preparation Time: 12 minutes

Cooking Time: about 5 hours

Servings: 12

Smoke Temperature: 225°F, 375°F

Preferred Wood Pellet: Hickory or Apple

Ingredients:

Minced garlic—1 tbsp.

Pork neck—1 1/2 lbs.

Cornstarch—1 tsp.

Salt—1 tsp.

Chicken stock—1 quart

Bacon—3 slices, chopped

Hot sauce—2 tsps.

Northwest beans—2 cans

Fresh parsley—1 tbsp., diced

Cold water—1 tsp.

Yellow onion—1 large, diced

Directions:

Prepare your Smoker grill by preheating it for the smoking process, keeping the lid open.

Use salt and pepper to season the pork neck and transfer it to the grilling grate. Smoke for about 2 hours. Set aside the meat to let it cool.

Use a large enough pot to heat onions in oil and season with salt and pepper.

Add pork neck, hot sauce, and more salt to the cooked onions. Add water and bring to a boil in the smoker-grill, then simmer.

Let the soup cook on simmer for about 3–4 hours without covering the lid. Then, take out the meat and allow it to cool. Once cooled, pull the meat and shred.

Add the shredded meat and beans back into the soup mixture and heat thoroughly.

Add a mixture of cornstarch and water and stir over medium-high heat. This will give the soup its desired consistency.

Serve with parsley and chopped bacon toppings.

Beef

10 Traeger BBQ Brisket

Preparation Time: 20 minutes

Cooking Time: 9 hours

Servings: 8-12

Smoke Temperature: 180°F and 375°F

Preferred Wood Pellet: Hickory

Ingredients:

1 (12-14 Lb.) Whole Packer Brisket

Traeger Beef Rub, As Needed

Directions:

Coat meat liberally with Traeger Beef Rub. When seasoned, wrap brisket in plastic wrap. Let the wrapped meat sit 12 to 24 hours in the refrigerator.

When ready to cook, set the Traeger to 225°F and preheat, lid closed for 15 minutes.

Place meat fat side down on the grill grate and cook for 6 hours or until internal Smoke Temperature reaches 160°F. Remove brisket from the grill and wrap in foil.

Place foiled brisket back on grill and cook until it reaches a finished internal Smoke Temperature of 204°F this should take an additional 3-4 hours.

Remove from grill and allow to rest in the foil for at least 30 minutes. Slice. Enjoy!

11 Garlic, Lemon, And Goat Cheese Mashed Potatoes

Preparation Time: 1 hour and 15 minutes

Cooking Time: 20 minutes

Servings: 6-8 servings

Smoke Temperature: 180°F and 375°F

Preferred Wood Pellet: Hickory

Ingredients:

1 Head of Garlic

1 Tsp Olive Oil

3 Lbs. Yukon Gold Potatoes, Peeled and Roughly Chopped

3/4 Cup Crumbled Goat Cheese

1/4 Cup Melted Butter, Plus More for Drizzling

3/4 Cup Heavy Whipping Cream

Sea Salt & Freshly Cracked Black Pepper

2 Tbs Fresh Chives, Finely Diced

Directions:

When ready to cook, set the Smoke Temperature to 350°F and preheat, lid closed, for 10 to 15 minutes.

Using a sharp knife, slice about ⅛" off the top of the garlic head (leaving the root intact), exposing the individual garlic cloves. Drizzle the olive oil on top of the exposed garlic and season with a pinch of salt and pepper. Tightly wrap the bulb in aluminum foil and roast on the Traeger for 30 - 35 minutes, until the cloves are soft. Remove the garlic cloves and mash into a paste with a fork.

Meanwhile, bring a large stockpot of salted water to a boil over medium high heat. Add the potatoes and cook for 15 - 20 minutes, or until softened and hashable. Drain and return to the pot, stirring until dry. Remove from Preferred Wood Pellet and stir in the cream, goat cheese, lemon zest, garlic mash, and ¼ cup of butter. Mash until smooth, and if you like it, whip that business up with a whisk. Season with salt and pepper to taste. Garnish with extra chives and a generous drizzle of melted butter. Enjoy!

12 Traeger Prime Rib Roast

Preparation Time: 20 minutes

Cooking Time: 3 hours

Servings: 10

Smoke Temperature: 180°F and 375°F

Preferred Wood Pellet: Hickory

Ingredients:

1 (5-7 Bones) Prime Rib Roast

Traeger Prime Rib Rub, As Needed

Directions:

Coat the roast evenly with the Traeger Prime Rib Rub and wrap in plastic wrap. Let sit in the refrigerator for 24 hours.

When ready to cook, set the Smoke Temperature to High and preheat, lid closed for 15 minutes.

Place the prime rib fat side up, directly on the grill grate and cook for 30 minutes. Starting at a higher heat will help to develop a crispy, rendered crust.

After 30 minutes, reduce the grill Smoke Temperature to 325°F.

Close lid and roast at 325°F for 3-4 hours or until cooked to desired internal Smoke Temperature, 120°F for rare, 130°F for medium rare, 140°F for medium and 150°F for well done.

Remove from grill and let rest 15 minutes before carving. Enjoy!

13 Italian Beef Sandwich

Preparation Time: 5 minutes

Cooking Time: 4 hours and 15 minutes

Servings: 8 servings

Smoke Temperature: 180°F and 375°F

Preferred Wood Pellet: Hickory

Ingredients:

1 Qty. (4 Lb.) Lean, Boneless Beef Roast (Sirloin or Top Round)

Salt

Pepper

4 Cloves Garlic, Thinly Sliced

Traeger Prime Rib Rub

6 Cups Beef Broth

8 Hoagie-Style Buns (For Sandwiches)

6 Slices Swiss cheese

1 Cup Bottled Giardiniera (Italian Pickled Vegetables; Optional), Chopped

Directions:

When ready to cook, set the Smoke Temperature to 450°F and preheat, lid closed for 15 minutes.

Season the roast liberally with salt, pepper and Traeger prime rib rub. Using a paring knife, make 10-15 slits in the roast every 1" or so. Insert a garlic clove into each slit.

Place the roast directly on the grill grate and cook for about 1 hour flipping halfway through until browned well.

Remove the roast from the grill and transfer to a deep Dutch oven. Pour the beef broth over the roast. Cover tightly with foil and place back on the grill. Reduce the grill Smoke Temperature to 300°F and cook the roast for 3-4 hours or until it is fork tender.

While the roast cooks, chop the giardiniera into small pieces.

Remove the Dutch oven from the grill and shred removing any significant bits of fat or connective tissue. Transfer the meat back to the Dutch over and stir to combine with the juices.

Increase the grill Smoke Temperature to high and preheat lid closed for 10 minutes.

Place hoagie buns cut side up on a small sheet tray. Fill with the shredded roast and top with a slice of cheese. Transfer to the grill and cook for another 5-10 minutes or until the cheese is melted.

Remove from the grill and top with chopped pickled veggies. Serve with remaining cooking liquid for dipping if desired. Enjoy!

14 Thai Beef Skewers

Preparation Time: 1 hour

Cooking Time: 10 minutes

Servings: 16 servings

Smoke Temperature: 180°F and 375°F

Preferred Wood Pellet: Hickory

Ingredients:

1/4 Cup Vegetable Oil

1/4 Cup Soy Sauce

1 Juice of Lime

2 Cloves Garlic, Finely Minced

1 Tbsp. Fresh Ginger, Peeled and Minced

1 Tbsp. Sugar

1 Tsp. Black Pepper, Freshly Ground

1/2 Beef Sirloin, Trimmed and Cut into 1-1/4 Inch Dice

1/2 Red Bell Pepper, Stemmed, Seeded, and Cut into 1/4 Inch Dice

1/2 Cup Dry-Roasted Peanuts (Salted or Unsalted), Coarsely Chopped

1 Traeger Skewers Set

Directions:

In a small bowl, whisk together the oil, soy sauce, lime juice, garlic, ginger, sugar, and black pepper. Transfer the meat to a large bowl or resealable plastic bag and pour the marinade over the meat, turning to coat each piece thoroughly. Refrigerate for 2 to 4 hours, or longer if desired.

Drain the marinade off the sirloin cubes (discard the marinade) and pat them dry with paper towels. Thread the meat on the skewers, keeping the pieces close together to minimize exposure of the skewer to Preferred Wood Pellet. (You can also slip a folded length of aluminum foil under the exposed ends to protect them.)

When ready to cook, set the Smoke Temperature to 425°F and preheat, lid closed for 15 minutes.

Arrange the skewers on the grill grate and grill for 2 to 4 minutes per side, or until the desired degree of doneness is reached. To serve, sprinkle with the diced red pepper and the chopped peanuts. Enjoy!

Poultry

15 Natural White Smoked Chicken Breast

Preparation Time: 15 minutes

Cooking Time: 2 Hours 15 Minutes

Servings: 10 servings

Smoke Temperature: 180°F and 375°F

Preferred Wood Pellet: Mesquite, Oak

Ingredients:

Boneless Chicken breast (4.5-lbs., 2 -kg.)

Vegetable oil – 3 tablespoons

Chicken broth – ¼ cup

Worcestershire sauce – 2 tablespoons

Salt – ¾ tablespoon

Garlic powder – 1 ½ teaspoons

Onion powder – 1 ½ teaspoons

Bay leaf – ¾ teaspoon

Thyme – ¾ teaspoon

Sage – ¾ teaspoon

Black pepper – ¾ teaspoon

Salt – 2 tablespoons

Minced garlic – 3 tablespoons

Minced ginger – 1 tablespoon

Lemon juice – 3 tablespoons

Directions:

Pour vegetable oil and chicken broth into a bowl then season with Worcestershire sauce, salt, garlic powder, onion powder, bay leaf, thyme, sage, and black pepper. Stir the liquid until incorporated.

Fill an injector with the liquid mixture then inject the chicken breast at several places.

After that, combine the rub ingredients—salt, minced garlic, minced ginger, and lemon juice in a bowl. Stir the spices until well mixed.

Rub the chicken breast with the spice mixture then let it rest for an hour.

Next, plug the Pellet smoker and place inside the hopper. Turn the switch on.

Set the "Smoke" setting and Prepare the Smoker for indirect heat.

Once the Pellet smoker is ready, set the Smoke Temperature to 250°F (121°C) and place the chicken breast in the Smoker.

Smoke the chicken for 2 hours and once the internal Smoke Temperature has reached 165°F (74°C), remove the smoked chicken from the Smoker.

Quickly wrap the smoked chicken with aluminum foil then let it rest for approximately an hour or so.

After an hour, unwrap the smoked chicken then cut into thick slices.

Arrange the sliced smoked chicken on a serving dish then serve immediately.

Enjoy!

16 Barbecue Chicken

Preparation Time: 30 minutes

Cooking Time: 2 hours

Servings: 8

Smoke Temperature: 180°F and 375°F

Preferred Wood Pellet: Mesquite, Oak

Ingredients:

8 Chicken breasts

Two t. salt

Two c. barbecue sauce, divided

Two t. garlic powder

Two t. pepper

Directions:

Add Preferred Wood Pellet pellets to your smoker and follow your cooker's startup procedure. Preheat your smoker, with your lid closed, until it reaches 250.

Rub the chicken with the spices and lay in a roasting pan. Cover the chicken before placing them on the grill. For about two hours, let them smoke. It should reach 165. During the last 15 minutes, baste with a c. of barbecue sauce.

Serve with the rest of the sauce.

17 Whole Turkey

Preparation Time: 1 hour

Cooking Time: 6 hours

Servings: 8-6

Smoke Temperature: 180°F and 375°F

Preferred Wood Pellet: Mesquite, Oak

Ingredients:

Two t. thyme

Two t. sage

½ c. apple juice

One stick melted butter

¼ c. poultry seasoning

10-12-pound turkey

Directions:

Add Preferred Wood Pellet pellets to your smoker and follow your cooker's startup procedure. Preheat your smoker, with your lid closed, until it reaches 250.

Rub the oil and seasoning on the turkey. Get some in under the skin as well as inside.

Mix the thyme, sage, juice, and butter.

Place the turkey in a roasting pan, put it on the grill, cover, and cook 5-6 hours. Baste it every hour with the juice mixture. It should reach 165. Let it rest for 15-20 minutes before carving.

18 Barbecue Chicken Breasts

Preparation Time: 15 minutes

Cooking Time: 30 minutes

Servings: 4

Smoke Temperature: 180°F and 375°F

Preferred Wood Pellet: Mesquite, Oak

Ingredients:

Two T. Worcestershire sauce

½ c. hot barbecue sauce

One c. barbecue sauce

Two cloves minced garlic

¼ c. olive oil

4 chicken breasts

Directions:

Put the chicken breasts into a deep container.

In another bowl, put the Worcestershire sauce, barbecue sauces, garlic, and olive oil. Stir well to combine.

Use half to marinate the chicken and reserve the rest for basting.

Add Preferred Wood Pellet pellets to your smoker and follow your cooker's startup procedure. Preheat your smoker, with your lid closed, until it reaches 350.

Take the chicken breasts out of the sauce. On the grill, place them before smoking them for approximately 20 minutes.

About ten minutes before the chicken is finished, baste with reserved barbecue sauce.

19 Cilantro-Lime Chicken

Preparation Time: 1 hour

Cooking Time: 4 hours

Servings: 4

Smoke Temperature: 180°F and 375°F

Preferred Wood Pellet: Mesquite, Oak

Ingredients:

Pepper

Salt

4 cloves minced garlic

½ c. lime juice

One c. honey

Two T. olive oil

½ c. chopped cilantro

4 chicken breasts

Directions:

Put the chicken breasts into a large zip-top bag.

In another bowl, put the pepper, salt, olive oil, garlic, honey, lime juice, and cilantro. Stir well to combine.

Use half as a marinade and reserve the rest for later.

Place into the refrigerator for four to five hours.

Add Preferred Wood Pellet pellets to your smoker and follow your cooker's startup procedure. Preheat your smoker, with your lid closed, until it reaches 350.

Remove the chicken breasts the bag. Use paper towels to pat them dry. Let them smoke up in the grill for about fifteen mins.

About five minutes before the chicken is finished, baste with reserved marinade.

20 Lemon Honey Chicken

Preparation Time: 10 minutes

Cooking Time: 45 minutes

Servings: 4

Smoke Temperature: 180°F and 375°F

Preferred Wood Pellet: Mesquite, Oak

Ingredients:

Pepper

Salt

Chopped rosemary

One clove crushed garlic

One T. honey

Juice of one lemon

½ c. chicken broth

3 T. butter

4 chicken breasts

Directions:

Place a pan on the stove and melt the butter. Place chicken breasts into hot butter and sear on each side until a nice color has formed.

Take out of the pan and allow resting for ten minutes.

In a small bowl, put the pepper, salt, rosemary, garlic, honey, lemon juice, and broth. Stir well to combine.

Rub each breast with the honey lemon mixture.

Add Preferred Wood Pellet pellets to your smoker and follow your cooker's startup procedure. Preheat your smoker, with your lid closed, until it reaches 350.

Put the chicken breasts onto the preheated grill and grill for 20 minutes.

21 Herbed Coffee Chicken

Preparation Time: 40 minutes

Cooking Time: 2 hours

Servings: 4

Smoke Temperature: 180°F and 375°F

Preferred Wood Pellet: Mesquite, Oak

Ingredients:

Salt

¾ c. strong brewed coffee

One t. coriander seeds

4 lemon slices

One t. peppercorns

One t. mustard seeds

½ c. chicken broth

¼ c. dark brown sugar, packed

Two T. melted butter

4 chicken breast halves

Directions:

Rub the butter on the chicken and rub in the salt.

In an enormous container, stir together the remaining ingredients. Cover the chicken with marinade.

Place into the refrigerator for two hours.

Add Preferred Wood Pellet pellets to your smoker and follow your cooker's startup procedure. Preheat your smoker, with your lid closed, until it reaches 350.

Smoke the chicken for ten minutes. There is no need to flip. Serve.

22 Red Pepper Chicken Thighs

Preparation Time: 45 minutes

Cooking Time: 4 hours

Servings: 6

Smoke Temperature: 180°F and 375°F

Preferred Wood Pellet: Mesquite, Oak

Ingredients:

One T. garlic powder

One t. curry powder

One t. red pepper flakes

One t. black pepper

Two T. olive oil

½ c. chicken broth

One t. oregano

One t. paprika

Two pounds chicken thighs

Directions:

Put the chicken thighs into a large flat dish in a single layer.

In a bowl, put the olive oil, garlic powder, curry, oregano, pepper, paprika, red pepper flakes, and broth. Stir well to combine.

The mixture should be poured on top of the chicken.

Let the chicken marinate for four hours.

Add Preferred Wood Pellet pellets to your smoker and follow your cooker's startup procedure. Preheat your smoker, with your lid closed, until it reaches 450.

The chicken thighs should be removed from the bag. Use paper towels to pat them dry. Place them onto the preheated grill with the skin down and smoke for ten minutes. Turnover and cook for an additional ten minutes.

23 Spicy Chicken Thighs

Preparation Time: 45 minutes

Cooking Time: 4 hours

Servings: 6

Smoke Temperature: 180°F and 375°F

Preferred Wood Pellet: Mesquite, Oak

Ingredients:

One T. dry barbecue spice

One t. coriander

One T. oregano

1/3 c. balsamic vinegar

Salt

Two T. mustard

1/3 c. olive oil

Pepper

Two cloves minced garlic

6 chicken thighs

Directions:

Put the chicken thighs into a shallow dish in one layer.

In a bowl, put the dry barbecue spice, coriander, oregano, pepper, salt, mustard, olive oil, balsamic vinegar, and garlic. Stir well to combine.

Use the mixture to coat the chicken.

Place into the refrigerator for four hours.

Add Preferred Wood Pellet pellets to your smoker and follow your cooker's startup procedure. Preheat your smoker, with your lid closed, until it reaches 350.

Remove the thighs of the chicken from the dish and use paper towels to pat them dry. Place them onto the preheated grill with the skin down and smoke for ten minutes. Flip them and cook an additional ten minutes.

24 Turkey Burgers

Preparation Time: 10 minutes

Cooking Time: 30 minutes

Servings: 6

Smoke Temperature: 180°F and 375°F

Preferred Wood Pellet: Mesquite, Oak

Ingredients:

½ t. oregano

½ t. thyme

Pepper

Salt

One large egg

½ bunch chopped parsley

Two pounds ground turkey

One small chopped red bell pepper

One finely chopped onion

Directions:

Put all ingredients into a large bowl.

Use your hands and mix all ingredients until combined well.

Make six patties. You can dip your hands into the water if the meat begins sticking to your hands.

Add Preferred Wood Pellet pellets to your smoker and follow your cooker's startup procedure. Preheat your smoker, with your lid closed, until it reaches 350.

Place them on the grill and smoke for five minutes, covered, until grill marks form. Turn each burger over and cook for an additional five minutes.

Check to see if the internal Smoke Temperature of the burgers has reached 165.

Serve with favorite burger toppings.

Fish & Seafood

25 Bacon Grilled Crappie

Preparation Time: 10 Minutes

Cooking Time: 3 Minutes

Servings: 5

Smoke Temperature: 180°F and 375°F

Preferred Wood Pellet: Mesquite, Oak

Ingredients:

20 Crappie Fillets

20 Bacon Slices

¼ teaspoon garlic powder

¼ teaspoon onion powder

¼ teaspoon pepper

Directions:

Sprinkle spices on fillets. Roll up fillets, wrap with bacon and peg with a toothpick.

Grill over meager heat, with apple Preferred Wood Pellet pellets, turning fillets several times.

Be sure to put out all flames caused by bacon grease with a water spray bottle.

Cook until bacon is brown and inside of fillet flakes.

26 Mojo Shrimp Skewer Appetizers

Preparation Time: 10 Minutes

Cooking Time: 6 Minutes

Servings: 32

Smoke Temperature: 180°F and 375°F

Preferred Wood Pellet: Mesquite, Oak

Ingredients:

2 lbs. sliced bacon

64 raw prawns, tail off

2 C Traditional Cuban Mojo

¼ C Adobo Criollo

32 Preferred Wood Pellet skewers, soaked

Directions:

Rinse raw prawns and drain. In a large bowl, toss prawns and Adobo Criollo spices.

Wrap each prawn in ½ slice of bacon, and thread two wraps onto each skewer, touching, and with skewer through both the bacon and the shrimp.

Bring pellet grill to medium heat, oil, and lay skewers in grill.

Grill 3-5 minutes, until bacon is cooked, flip, and cook 2-3 more minutes.

Remove from grill and let rest on a paper-towel covered platters 2-3 minutes before serving. for this type of grilling.

27 Sweet Grilled Lobster Tails

Preparation Time: 10 Minutes

Cooking Time: 7 Minutes

Servings: 12

Smoke Temperature: 180°F and 375°F

Preferred Wood Pellet: Mesquite, Oak

Ingredients:

12 lobster tails

½ C olive oil

¼ C fresh lemon juice

½ C butter

1 Tbsp. crushed garlic

1 tsp sugar

1/2 tsp salt

½ tsp black pepper

Directions:

Combine lemon juice, butter, garlic, salt, and pepper over med-low heat and mix until well blended, keep warm.

Create a "cool zone" at one end of the pellet grill. Brush the meat side of tails with olive oil, place onto grill and cook for 5-7 minutes, depending on the size of the lobster tail.

Make sure to turn once during cooking process.

After turning, baste meat with garlic butter 2-3 times.

The shell should be bright red when they are finished. Remove the tails from the grill, and using large kitchen shears, cut the top part of the shell open.

Serve with warm garlic butter for dipping.

28 Seasoned Smoked Oysters

Preparation Time: 20 minutes

Cooking Time: 1½-2 hours

Servings: 2 dozen

Smoke Temperature: 225°F

Preferred Wood Pellet: Alder, Hickory or Oak

Ingredients:

1-gallon cold water

½ cup soy sauce

2 tablespoons Worcestershire sauce

1 cup salt

1 cup firmly packed brown sugar

2 dried bay leaves

2 garlic cloves, minced

2 teaspoons freshly ground black pepper

1 tablespoon hot sauce

1 tablespoon onion powder

2 dozen raw, shucked oysters, shells discarded

¼ cup olive oil

½ cup (1 stick) unsalted butter, at room Smoke Temperature

1 teaspoon garlic powder

Crackers or toast points, for serving

Cocktail sauce, for serving

Directions:

In a large container, mix the water, soy sauce, Worcestershire, salt, sugar, bay leaves, garlic, pepper, hot sauce, and onion powder.

Submerge the raw oysters in the brine, cover the container, and refrigerate overnight.

Following the manufacturer's specific start-up procedure, preheat the smoker to 225°F, and add alder, hickory, or oak Preferred Wood Pellet.

Remove the oysters from the refrigerator, discarding the brine, and rinse them thoroughly.

Place the oysters on a nonstick grill mat, drizzle with the olive oil, and place the mat in the smoker.

Smoke the oysters for 1½ to 2 hours, until firm. Meanwhile, in a small bowl, stir together the butter and garlic powder.

Remove the oysters from Preferred Wood Pellet, and drizzle with the seasoned butter.

Serve the oysters with the crackers or toast points and cocktail sauce.

29 Sugar-Crusted Red Snapper

Preparation Time: 10 minutes

Cooking Time: 1 TO 1½ hours

Servings: 2

Smoke Temperature: 225°F

Preferred Wood Pellet: Alder

Ingredients:

1 tablespoon brown sugar

2 teaspoons minced garlic

2 teaspoons salt

2 teaspoons freshly ground black pepper

½ teaspoon crushed red pepper flakes

1 (1½- to 2-pound) red snapper fillet

2 tablespoons olive oil, plus more for oiling the grate

1 sliced lime, for garnish

Directions:

Following the manufacturer's specific start-up procedure, preheat the smoker to 225°F, and add alder Preferred Wood Pellet.

In a small bowl, mix the brown sugar, garlic, and salt, pepper, and red pepper flakes to make a spice blend.

Rub the olive oil all over the fish and apply the spice blend to coat.

Oil the grill grate or a nonstick grill mat or perforated pizza screen. Place the fillet on the smoker rack and smoke for 1 to 1½ hours, until the internal Smoke Temperature registers 145°F.

Remove the fish from Preferred Wood Pellet and serve hot with the lime slices.

30 Peppercorn-Dill Mahi-Mahi

Preparation Time: 10 minutes

Cooking Time: 1 to 1½ hours

Servings: 4

Smoke Temperature: 225°F

Preferred Wood Pellet: Alder or Pecan

Ingredients:

4 mahi-mahi fillets

¼ cup chopped fresh dill

2 tablespoons freshly squeezed lemon juice

1 tablespoon crushed black peppercorns

2 teaspoons minced garlic

1 teaspoon onion powder

1 teaspoon salt

2 tablespoons olive oil, plus more for oiling the grate

Directions:

Following the manufacturer's specific start-up procedure, preheat the smoker to 225°F, and add alder or pecan Preferred Wood Pellet.

Trim the fillets as needed, cutting out any visible red bloodline. It will not hurt you, but its more robust flavor can quickly permeate the rest of the fillet.

In a small bowl, whisk together the dill, lemon juice, peppercorns, garlic, onion powder, and salt to make a seasoning.

Rub the fish with the olive oil and apply the seasoning all over. Oil the grill grate or a nonstick grill mat or perforated pizza screen.

Place the fillets on the smoker rack and smoke for 1 to 1½ hours, until the flesh is opaque and the internal Smoke Temperature registers 145°F.

Remove the fillets from Preferred Wood Pellet and serve hot.

31 Fish Tacos with Sweet and Fiery Peppers

Preparation Time: 15 minutes

Cooking Time: 1 hour

Servings: 4

Smoke Temperature: 225°F

Preferred Wood Pellet: Apricot or Alder

Ingredients:

1 (16-ounce) carton prepared sweet coleslaw

1 small red onion, chopped

1 poblano pepper, chopped

1 jalapeño pepper, chopped

1 serrano pepper, chopped

¼ cup chopped fresh cilantro

1 tablespoon minced garlic

2 teaspoons salt, divided

2 teaspoons freshly ground black pepper, divided

1 lime, halved

1-pound skinless cod, halibut, or any white fish (see tip)

1 tablespoon olive oil, plus more for oiling the grate

Flour or corn tortillas

1 avocado, sliced thin

Directions:

In a medium bowl, stir together the coleslaw, onion, poblano, jalapeño, serrano, cilantro, garlic, and 1 teaspoon each of salt and pepper to make a sweet hot-pepper slaw. Refrigerate the slaw until ready to serve.

Following the manufacturer's specific start-up procedure, preheat the smoker to 225°F, and add apricot or alder Preferred Wood Pellet.

Juice one half of the lime and cut the other half into wedges.

Rub the fish all over with the lime juice and olive oil.

Season the fish with the remaining 1 teaspoon each of salt and pepper. Oil the grill grate or a nonstick grill mat or perforated pizza screen.

Place the fish on the smoker rack and smoke for 1 to 1½ hours

Five to 10 minutes before the end of the cook, place the tortillas on a damp paper towel. Wrap the tortillas in heavy-duty aluminum foil with the towel. Seal the foil tightly and place on the smoker rack.

Remove the fish and tortillas from Preferred Wood Pellet when the fish is flaky and opaque and the internal Smoke Temperature registers 145°F.

Cut the fish into small chunks. Serve the fish pieces with the tortillas, avocado slices, and sweet hot-pepper slaw.

32 Honey-Cayenne Sea Scallops

Preparation Time: 10 minutes

Cooking Time: 25 minutes

Servings: 4

Smoke Temperature: 225°F

Preferred Wood Pellet: Oak or Cherry

Ingredients:

½ cup (1 stick) butter, melted

¼ cup honey

2 tablespoons ground cayenne pepper

1 tablespoon brown sugar

1 teaspoon garlic powder

1 teaspoon onion powder

½ teaspoon salt

20 sea scallops (about 2 pounds)

Directions:

Following the manufacturer's specific start-up procedure, preheat the smoker to 225°F, and add oak or cherry Preferred Wood Pellet.

In a small bowl, whisk together the butter, honey, cayenne, brown sugar, garlic powder, onion powder, and salt.

Place the scallops in a disposable aluminum foil roasting pan and pour the seasoned honey butter over them.

Set the pan on the smoker rack and smoke the scallops for about 25 minutes, until opaque and firm and the internal Smoke Temperature registers 130°F.

Remove the scallops from Preferred Wood Pellet and serve hot.

Vegetables

33 Smoked Vegetable "Potpourri" (Pellet)

Preparation Time: 15 minutes

Cooking Time: 1 hour

Servings: 6

Smoke Temperature: 180°F and 375°F

Preferred Wood Pellet: Maple

Ingredients:

2 large zucchinis sliced

2 red bell peppers sliced

2 Russet potatoes sliced

1 red onion sliced

1/2 cup of olive oil

Salt and ground black pepper to taste

Directions:

Start the pellet grill on SMOKE with the lid open until the fire is established. Set the Smoke Temperature to 350 °F and preheat, lid closed, for 10 to 15 minutes.

In the meantime, rinse and slice all vegetables, pat dry on a kitchen paper.

Generously season with the salt and pepper, and drizzle with olive oil.

Place your sliced vegetables into grill basket or onto grill rack and smoke for 40 to 45 minutes.

Serve hot.

34 Perfectly Smoked Artichoke Hearts

Preparation Time: 10 minutes

Cooking Time: 2 hours

Servings: 6

Smoke Temperature: 180°F and 375°F

Preferred Wood Pellet: Maple

Ingredients:

12 canned whole artichoke hearts

1/4 cup of extra virgin olive oil

4 cloves of garlic minced

2 Tbsp of fresh parsley finely chopped (leaves)

1 Tbsp of fresh lemon juice freshly squeezed

Salt to taste

Lemon for garnish

Directions:

Start the pellet grill on SMOKE with the lid open until the fire is established. Set the Smoke Temperature to 350 °F and preheat, lid closed, for 10 to 15 minutes.

In a bowl, combine all remaining ingredients and pour over artichokes.

Place artichokes on a grill rack and smoke for 2 hours or so.

Serve hot with extra olive oil, and lemon halves.

35 Finely Smoked Russet Potatoes

Preparation Time: 15 minutes

Cooking Time: 2 hours

Servings: 6

Smoke Temperature: 180°F and 375°F

Preferred Wood Pellet: Maple

Ingredients:

8 large Russet potatoes

1/2 cup of garlic-infused olive oil

Kosher salt and black pepper to taste

Directions:

Start the pellet grill on SMOKE with the lid open until the fire is established. Set the Smoke Temperature to 225 °F and preheat, lid closed, for 10 to 15 minutes.

Rinse and dry your potatoes, pierce with a fork on all sides.

Drizzle with garlic-infused olive oil and rub generously all your potatoes with the salt and pepper.

Place the potatoes on the pellet smoker and close the lid.

Smoke potatoes for about 2 hours.

Serve hot with your favorite dressing.

36 Simple Smoked Green Cabbage (Pellet)

Preparation Time: 55 minutes

Cooking Time: 1 hour

Servings: 4

Smoke Temperature: 180°F and 375°F

Preferred Wood Pellet: Maple

Ingredients:

1 medium head of green cabbage

1/2 cup of olive oil

salt and ground white pepper to taste

Directions:

Start the pellet grill on SMOKE with the lid open until the fire is established. Set the Smoke Temperature to 250 °F and preheat, lid closed, for 10 to 15 minutes.

Clean and rinse cabbage under running water.

Cut the stem and then cut it in half, then each half in 2 to 3 pieces.

Season generously cabbage with the salt and white ground pepper, drizzle with olive oil.

Arrange the cabbage peace on their side on a smoker tray and cover.

Smoke the cabbage for 20 minutes per side.

Remove cabbage and let rest for 5 minutes.

Serve immediately.

37 Smoked Asparagus with Parsley and Garlic

Preparation Time: 10 minutes

Cooking Time: 1 hour

Servings: 3

Smoke Temperature: 180°F and 375°F

Preferred Wood Pellet: Maple

Ingredients:

1 bunch of fresh asparagus, cleaned

1 Tbs of finely chopped parsley

1 Tbs of minced garlic

1/2 cup of olive oil

Salt and ground black pepper to taste

Directions:

Start the pellet grill on SMOKE with the lid open until the fire is established. Set the Smoke Temperature to 225 °F and preheat, lid closed, for 10 to 15 minutes.

Rinse and cut the ends off the asparagus.

In a bowl, combine olive oil, chopped parsley, minced garlic, and the salt and pepper.

Season your asparagus with olive oil mixture.

Place the asparagus on a heavy-duty foil and fold the sides.

Smoke for 55 to 60 minutes or until soft (turn every 15 minutes).

Serve hot.

38 Smoked Corn Cob with Spicy Rub

Preparation Time: 40 minutes

Cooking Time: 1 hour

Servings: 4

Smoke Temperature: 180°F and 375°F

Preferred Wood Pellet: Maple

Ingredients:

10 ears of fresh sweet corn on the cob

1/2 cup of macadamia nut oil

Kosher salt and fresh ground black pepper to taste

1/2 tsp of garlic powder

1/2 tsp of hot paprika flakes

1/2 tsp of dried parsley

1/4 tsp of ground mustard

Directions:

Start the pellet grill on SMOKE with the lid open until the fire is established. Set the Smoke Temperature to 350 °F and preheat, lid closed, for 10 to 15 minutes.

Combine macadamia nut oil with garlic powder, hot paprika flakes, dried parsley, and ground mustard.

Rub your corn with macadamia nut oil mixture and place on a grill rack.

Smoke corn for 80 to 90 minutes.

Serve hot.

39 Smoked Sweet Pie Pumpkins

Preparation Time: 2 hours

Cooking Time: 1 hour

Servings: 6

Smoke Temperature: 180°F and 375°F

Preferred Wood Pellet: Maple

Ingredients:

4 small pie pumpkins

avocado oil to taste

Directions:

Start the pellet grill on SMOKE with the lid open until the fire is established. Set the Smoke Temperature to 250 °F and preheat, lid closed, for 10 to 15 minutes.

Cut pumpkins in half, top to bottom, and drizzle with avocado oil.

Place pumpkin halves on the smoker away from the fire.

Smoke pumpkins from 1 1/2 to 2 hours.

Remove pumpkins from smoked and allow to cool.

Serve to taste.

Other Meats

40 Wild Game Chili

Preparation Time: 50 minutes

Cooking Time: 6 hours

Servings: 8-12 servings

Smoke Temperature: 180°F and 375°F

Preferred Wood Pellet: Maple

Ingredients:

3 slices of bacon, chopped

Venison or wild hog, ground into small cubes (3-lb, 1.4-kgs)

1 large onion, peeled, finely chopped

Beer (1-qt, 0.9-lt)

Canned chopped green chilies (4-oz, 113-gms)

Cumin seeds, crushed – 1 tablespoon

Chili seasoning mix, of choice – ⅔ cup

Tomato juice (1-qt, 0.9-lt)

Hot pepper sauce – 1 tablespoon

White cornmeal – ½ cup

Directions:

In a frying pan, sauté the bacon with the onions, until the bacon is just browned.

Add the game and sear all over.

In a pan, add 1½ cups of beer along with the green chilies, cumin, and chili mix, simmering until it is a gravy-like consistency.

Add the remaining beer followed by the tomato juice and hot pepper sauce.

Pour the mixture into a pan and transfer to the smoker.

Smoke-cook for between 4-6 hours.

Before serving, add the cornmeal and stir to thicken and combine.

Simmer for 20 minutes and serve with flour tortillas.

41 Mesquite Bison Brisket

Preparation Time: 25 minutes

Cooking Time: 4 hours

Servings: 6-8

Smoke Temperature: 225°F

Preferred Wood Pellet: mesquite

Ingredients:

1 (3-pound) bison brisket (see tip)

2 tablespoons olive oil

¼ cup All-Purpose Meat Rub

2 cups Perfection Spray and Mop Sauce, divided

2 tablespoons salt

¼ cup Hot Pepper Vinegar Sauce, for serving

¼ cup Bluesy Competition BBQ Sauce, for serving

Directions:

Place the brisket on a plate, rub with olive oil, and coat well with the All-Purpose Meat Rub.

Cover the plate loosely with plastic wrap. Refrigerate the brisket overnight to dry brine.

Following the manufacturer's specific start-up procedure, preheat the smoker to 225°F, and add mesquite Preferred Wood Pellet.

Remove the brisket from the refrigerator, but do not rinse it.

In a small bowl, whisk together 1 cup of Perfection Spray and Mop Sauce and the salt to make an injection sauce.

Fill a meat injector with the injection sauce. Inject the brisket with the sauce in several spots along the top and sides. Do not inject the bottom, as it will run out.

Place the brisket on the smoker rack and smoke for 2 hours.

Pour the remaining 1 cup of Perfection Spray into a plastic spray bottle.

Remove the brisket from the smoker. Wrap it in heavy-duty aluminum foil (or butcher paper). Spray about half of the Perfection Spray all over the meat before tightly sealing the foil.

Return the brisket to the smoker and smoke it for about 2 more hours, or until the internal Smoke Temperature registers 190°F.

Remove the brisket from Preferred Wood Pellet and spray it with the remaining Perfection Spray. Let the meat rest for 15 to 20 minutes.

In a small bowl, stir together the Hot Pepper Vinegar Sauce and Bluesy Competition BBQ Sauce until well combined. Feel free to use one or the other, instead of combining them—just remember that the vinegar sauce is hot. Serve the bison with the sauce(s).

42 Grilled Lamb Chops with Herbed Brown Sugar Marinade

Preparation Time: 2 hours

Cooking Time: 20 minutes

Servings: 4

Smoke Temperature: 180°F and 375°F

Preferred Wood Pellet: Maple

Ingredients:

4 lamb chops

1/4 cup brown sugar

1 tsp garlic powder

2 tsp ground ginger

2 tsp dried tarragon

1 tsp ground cinnamon

Salt and ground black pepper to taste

Directions:

Mix brown sugar, ginger, tarragon, cinnamon, pepper, garlic powder, and salt in a bowl. Rub lamb chops with the brown sugar mix, and place in a deep.

Cover, and refrigerate for 2 hours (preferably overnight).

Set the Smoke Temperature to HIGH (450F) and preheat, lid closed, for 10 to 15 minutes.

Remove the lamb chops from marinade and place directly on grill grate.

Grill for 10 to 15 minutes per side (135F internal Smoke Temperature for medium-rare).

Serve hot with your favorite vegetables or salad.

43 Grilled Orange-Turmeric Lamb Skewers

Preparation Time: 20 minutes

Cooking Time: 20 minutes

Servings: 4

Smoke Temperature: 180°F and 375°F

Preferred Wood Pellet: Maple

Ingredients:

1 lb. boneless lamb meat, boneless cut into 1/2" cubes

Marinade

2 tbsp orange juice

1 cup plain low-fat yogurt

1/4 tsp ground ginger

1/2 tsp turmeric

1/2 tsp ground cumin

1 tbsp ground coriander

1/2 tsp salt

Skewers

Directions:

Cut boneless lamb meat into 1/2" cubes.

Whisk together all ingredients from the list in a large bowl.

Add the lamb meat cubes to the bowl and stir to coat with the marinade evenly. Cover and refrigerate overnight.

Remove the bowl with marinated lamb 15 - 20 minutes before grilling.

Start the pellet grill to pre-heat with the lid open until the fire is established; about 5 minutes. Set the Smoke Temperature to High and preheat, lid closed, for 10 to 15 minutes.

Remove the meat from the marinade, pat lightly with paper towels to dry. Place meat evenly on the skewers.

Perfectly grilled lamb chops skewers will take about 4 - 5 minutes on each side.

Serve hot.

44 Grilled Rabbit with Wine and Rosemary Marinade

Preparation Time: 10 minutes

Cooking Time: 40 minutes

Servings: 6

Smoke Temperature: 180°F and 375°F

Preferred Wood Pellet: Maple

Ingredients:

1 rabbit cut into pieces

For marinade

3 cloves of garlic, mashed

1 1/2 tsp rosemary

1 cup of white wine, dry

1/2 cup olive oil

1 tbsp white vinegar

1 tsp mustard

1/2 tsp cumin

Salt and ground pepper to taste

Directions:

In a large bowl, whisk all marinade ingredients from the list.

Place the rabbit meat in marinade and toss to combine well.

Cover with plastic wrap and refrigerate for several hours (preferably overnight).

Remove meat from marinade and pat dry on a paper towel.

Set the Smoke Temperature to High and preheat your pellet grill, lid closed, for 10 to 15 minutes.

Place the rabbit pieces directly on grill rack.

Grill for about 12 to 15 minutes per side.

An instant-read meat thermometer inserted into the thickest part of a piece should read at least 160 degrees.

The rabbit meat is ready when no longer pink inside and the juices run clear.

Serve hot.

45 Grilled Wild Boar Steaks with Blueberry Sauce

Preparation Time: 40 minutes

Cooking Time: 1 hour

Servings: 6

Smoke Temperature: 180°F and 375°F

Preferred Wood Pellet: Maple

Ingredients:

4 large steaks of wild boar

For the marinade

2 glasses dry red wine

Juice from 1 lemon, preferably organic

2 bay leaves

2 tbsp sweet paprika powder

1 cup fresh celery, finely chopped

Salt and black pepper, crushed

1 tsp rosemary fresh or dry

For the sauce

3/4 lbs. blueberries

1 tsp brown sugar

Salt and white freshly ground pepper to taste

Directions:

Wash and wipe the wild boar steaks.

In a broad and deep pan, place all the ingredients for the marinade and mix well.

Submerge the wild boar steaks in marinade and refrigerate overnight.

The next day, drain the wild boar steaks (strain the marinade and set aside) and wipe them thoroughly with kitchen towels.

Start the pellet grill to pre-heat at 500 degrees, lid closed, for 10 to 15 minutes.

Place the steaks on grill and close lid and cook about (5) minutes on each side for medium steak, or 8-10 minutes for large steaks.

In the meantime, make a sauce: In a saucepan heat all the ingredients all sauce ingredients and bring to boil over medium heat. Boil for 2 minutes, stirring and remove from the fire.

Transfer the sauce to your blender and beat until smooth and creamy.

Serve the steaks immediately with the blueberry sauce.

Dessert

46 Apple Cobbler

Preparation Time: 30 minutes.

Cooking Time: 1 hour. 50 minutes.

Servings: 8

Smoke Temperature: 180°F and 375°F

Preferred Wood Pellet: Maple

Ingredients:

8 Granny Smith apples

One c. sugar

One stick melted butter

One t. cinnamon

Pinch salt

½ c. brown sugar

Two eggs

Two t. baking powder

Two c. plain flour

1 ½ c. sugar

Directions:

Peel and quarter apples, place into a bowl. Add in the cinnamon and one c. sugar. Stir well to coat and let it set for one hour.

Add Preferred Wood Pellet pellets to your smoker and follow your cooker's startup procedure. Preheat your smoker, with your lid closed, until it reaches 350.

In a large bowl add the salt, baking powder, eggs, brown sugar, sugar, and flour. Mix until it forms crumbles.

Place apples into a Dutch oven. Add the crumble mixture on top and drizzle with melted butter.

Place on the grill and cook for 50 minutes.

47 Pineapple Cake

Preparation Time: 30 minutes.

Cooking Time: 1 hour. 20 minutes.

Servings: 8

Smoke Temperature: 180°F and 375°F

Preferred Wood Pellet: Maple

Ingredients:

One c. sugar

One T. baking powder

One c. buttermilk

½ t. salt

One jar maraschino cherry

One stick butter, divided

¾ c. brown sugar

One can pineapple slice

1 ½ c. flour

Directions:

Add Preferred Wood Pellet pellets to your smoker and follow your cooker's startup procedure. Preheat your smoker, with your lid closed, until it reaches 350.

Take a medium-sized cast iron skillet and melt one half stick butter. Be sure to coat the entire skillet. Sprinkle brown sugar into a cast iron skillet.

Lay the sliced pineapple on top of the brown sugar. Put a cherry into each individual pineapple ring.

Mix the salt, baking powder, flour, and sugar. Add in the eggs, one-half stick melted butter, and buttermilk. Whisk to combine.

Put the cake on the grill and cook for an hour.

Take off from the grill and let it set for ten minutes. Flip onto serving platter.

48 Caramel Bananas

Preparation Time: 15 minutes.

Cooking Time: 15 minutes.

Servings: 4

Smoke Temperature: 180°F and 375°F

Preferred Wood Pellet: Maple

Ingredients:

1/3 c. chopped pecans

½ c. sweetened condensed milk

4 slightly green bananas

½ c. brown sugar

2 tbsp. corn syrup

½ c. butter

Directions:

Add pellet to your smoker and follow your cooker's startup procedure. Preheat your smoker, with the lid closed, until it reaches 350.

Place the milk, corn syrup, butter, and brown sugar into a heavy saucepan and bring to boil. For five mins., simmer the mixture in low heat. Stir frequently.

Place the bananas with their peels on, on the grill and let them grill for five minutes. Flip and cook for five minutes more. Peels will be dark and might split.

Place on serving platter. Cut the ends off the bananas and split peel down the middle. Take the peel off the bananas and spoon caramel on top. Sprinkle with pecans.

49 Exotic Apple Pie

Preparation Time: 20 minutes

Cooking Time: 1:30 Hours

Servings: 4

Smoke Temperature: 180°F and 375°F

Preferred Wood Pellet: Maple

Ingredients:

3 Apples (large, thinly sliced)

1/3 Cup of Sugar

1 Tablespoon of Flour

1/4 Teaspoon of Cinnamon (ground)

1 Tablespoon of Lemon juice

Pinch of Nutmeg (ground)

Pinch of salt

Homemade pie or box of pie dough

Directions:

Pepping for the Grill

Mix apples, flour, and sugar, cinnamon, nutmeg, salt, and lemon juice in a bowl thoroughly

Cut the dough into two

Put one half of the dough into the 10" pie plate and press firmly with your hand

Pour the apple mix into the dough and cover it with the other half

Use your hand again to crimp the edges of the pie together

Use knife cut the top of the dough

Pepping on the Pellet Smoker

Set the Smoker grill to indirect cooking and preheat to 425°F

Transfer to the smoker and bake, and then cover the edges of the pie with foil to avoid burn

Bake the dough until it turns golden brown approximately 45 minutes

Remove and allow cooling for 1 hour

Slice, serve and enjoy

50 Baked Peaches Pie

Preparation Time: 5 minutes

Cooking Time: 50 Minutes

Servings: 3

Smoke Temperature: 180°F and 375°F

Preferred Wood Pellet: Maple

Ingredients:

1 Cup of Rice peaches (peeled, sliced)

3/4 Cup of White sugar

1 Teaspoon of Baking powder

1/2 Cup of Milk (whole)

1/2 Cup of Flour

1/4 Teaspoon of Vanilla extract

1/4 Cup of salted butter (melted)

1/2 Cup of Blueberries (fresh)

1/4 teaspoon of salt

Directions:

Pepping for the Grill

Mix peaches, two-thirds of the sugar and blueberries in a bowl until the berries are fully coated

In another bowl blend flour, salt, baking powder, and the remaining sugar

Then add vanilla, milk, and the melted butter until well blended

Pour the dough into ungreased baking pan

Pour the coated blueberries on the dough evenly

Pepping on the Pellet Smoker

Set the Smoker grill to indirect cooking and preheat to 375°F

Transfer the batter to the smoker and bake until it turns firm and golden brown; approximately 50 minutes

Allow cooling for 10 minutes

Serve and enjoy while warm